WHAT'S INSIDE?
CLASSIC WARSHIPS

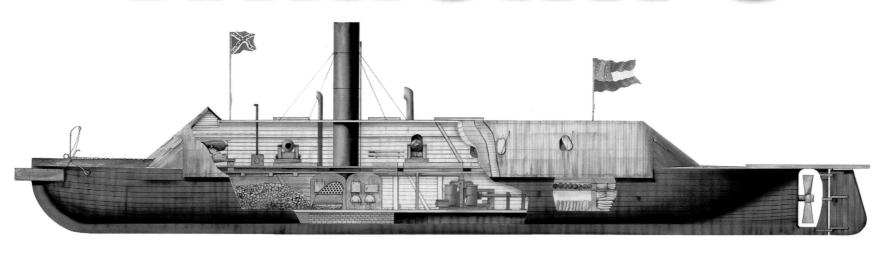

Peter Mavrikis

PowerKiDS
press™

WHAT'S INSIDE?
CLASSIC WARSHIPS

Peter Mavrikis

PowerKiDS press™

Published in 2016 by The Rosen Publishing Group, Inc.
29 East 21st Street, New York, NY 10010

Cataloging-in-Publication Data
Mavrikis, Peter.
Classic warships / by Peter Mavrikis.
p. cm. — (What's inside?)
Includes index.
ISBN 978-1-5081-4607-0 (pbk.)
ISBN 978-1-5081-4608-7 (6-pack)
ISBN 978-1-5081-4609-4 (library binding)
1. Warships — Juvenile literature.
2. Warships — Pictorial works — Juvenile literature.
I. Mavrikis, Peter. II. Title.
V765.M39 2016
623.825—d23

Project Editor: Sarah Uttridge
Design: Brian Rust and Andrew Easton
Picture Research: Terry Forshaw

Photographs:
AKG Images: 11 (IAM)
Alamy: 10 (MEPL), 12 (MEPL), 18 (Homes Garden Photos),
19 (Walker Art Library), 23 (Glasshouse Images), 31 (MEPL),
44 (Classic Image);
Art Archive: 14 (Cornelis de Vries)
Bridgeman Art Library/Peabody Essex Museum: 26, 28;
Cody Images: 34, 36, 43; Corbis: 22 (Gallery Collection)
Dreamstime: 20 (Michael Wood), 24 (Jon Helgason), 35 (Shutter 970)
Mary Evans Picture Library: 6, 8, 15, 16, 32;
Library of Congress: 3, 38, 39, 40
Public Domain: 7, 27, 30, 42

Artworks:
Art-Tech/Aerospace: 17, 29
Art-Tech/De Agostini: 1, 9, 13, 21, 25, 33, 37, 41, 45

Manufactured in the United States of America
CPSIA Compliance Information: Batch #BW16PK:
For Further Information contact Rosen Publishing, New York, New York at 1-800-237-9932

Contents

Henry Grace à Dieu (1514)

The warship *Henry Grace à Dieu* was built during the reign of King Henry VIII of England (1491–1547). Completed in 1514, she was the largest ship to sail the seas during the 16th century.

Often referred to as "Great Harry," this naval vessel was an English **carrack** and was mostly used to show off the wealth and power of Henry VIII.

First-Rate Ship

Henry Grace à Dieu weighed over 1,000 tons—or 2 million pounds (900,000 kg). She had four **masts**, each carrying large sails for added speed. Her **armament** included 21 heavy bronze cannons, along with a number of smaller iron cannons.

Henry Grace à Dieu **was 165 feet (50 m) long and had a number of cannons on decks along the ship.**

The two forward masts held large square sails that helped capture the power of the wind. The aft masts had lateen (triangular) sails.

The guns were placed on the deck, as well as below decks, and were fired through open **gun ports**. **Murder holes** were used by archers to fire arrows at enemy ships or to defend against foes boarding the vessel.

Did you know?

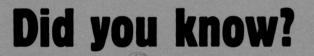

• *Henry Grace à Dieu* is French for "Henry, Grace of God."

• Construction of the ship started in 1512 and took two years to complete.

"Great Harry"

Although "Great Harry" saw limited action in battle, Henry VIII often used her on his diplomatic trips to France to display the strength of the English navy. *Henry Grace à Dieu* remained in the service of the English monarchy until an accidental fire destroyed the ship in 1553.

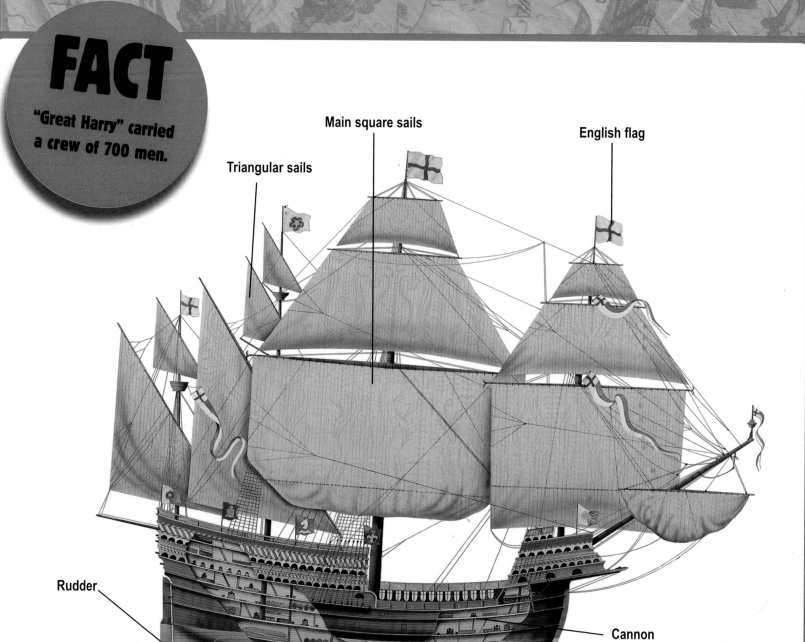

FACT

"Great Harry" carried a crew of 700 men.

Triangular sails

Main square sails

English flag

Rudder

Cannon

Sovereign of the Seas (1637)

Built on the orders of the British king, Charles I (1600–1649), *Sovereign of the Seas* was the largest and most expensive ship of her time.

Launched in 1637, she was the first ship built with three decks. *Sovereign of the Seas* was also heavily armed with over 100 main guns and numerous smaller cannons.

Breaking the Bank

At the time, most of the large, carrack-type ships had an average cost of £6,000—or more than $1 million in today's money. The final cost of Sovereign of the Seas was over ten times that amount. In addition to her size, the ship was also beautifully designed and richly decorated with many detailed engravings carved into the wood.

Like most ships of her time, *Sovereign of the Seas* relied on wind power for her source of propulsion.

The ship was 127 feet (39 m) long and weighed a little over 1,500 tons—more than 3 million pounds (1.3 million kg).

Triple-Decker

Sovereign of the Seas was the most powerful ship of her time. She was the first ship to be built with multiple decks. And she continued to rule the seas for years after the reign of Charles I had ended. Each deck was built with gun ports. The lower and middle decks each had 30 cannons, while the upper deck carried over 40.

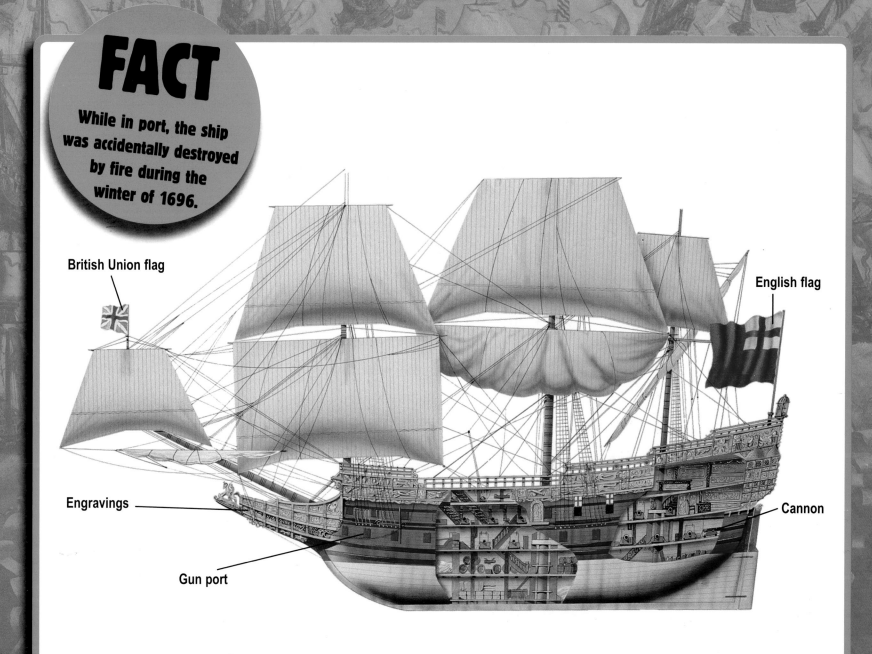

FACT

While in port, the ship was accidentally destroyed by fire during the winter of 1696.

British Union flag

English flag

Engravings

Cannon

Gun port

Le Soleil Royal (1669)

Built during the reign of French king Louis XIV (1638–1715), *Le Soleil Royal* was the flagship of the French fleet and a symbol of the king's power and wealth. Beautifully decorated with wooden carvings, the warship was also a powerful weapon that fought in many battles.

Armed with 104 heavy cannons and a number of smaller guns, *Le Soleil Royal* fought enemy ships in the Mediterranean Sea as well as the Atlantic Ocean.

Nine Years' War

Fought between France and an alliance of nations led by Britain and the Netherlands, the Nine Years' War started in 1688. The key to France's early success in the war were the naval battles in which

Le Soleil Royal was well known for its beautiful design and detailed woodwork. This drawing of the ship was included in a French manuscript.

Battle of Beachy Head

On July 10, 1690, flagship of the French fleet, *Le Soleil Royal*, led over 70 ships across the English Channel and to the coast of southern England. There they surprised a fleet of English and Dutch ships. The battle was a great victory for the French. Having managed to destroy close to a dozen enemy vessels, all the French ships returned to port safely.

Le Soleil Royal was 200 feet (61 m) long, and was fitted with three masts.

Le Soleil Royal played a crucial role. *Le Soleil Royal* destroyed a number of enemy ships in the French victory at Beachy Head in 1690. Another key win came at Barfleur. These victories helped ensure France's position as a power in Europe. The war ended in 1697 with favorable terms for France.

Did you know?

• In 1692, a combined Dutch and English force destroyed the defenseless *Le Soleil Royal* as she was being repaired in port.

• Though able to carry as many as 1,200 men, the standard size of the ship's crew was closer to 800.

FACT

Le Soleil Royal is French for "Royal Sun." King Louis XIV is also referred to as the "Sun King."

Rigging

Sail

Stern lamp

Captain's quarters

Hull

Boat

HMS Victory (1765)

HMS *Victory* is the oldest existing commissioned warship in the world. Having spent close to 250 years in the Royal Navy, this historic vessel remains the flagship of the British Royal Navy.

The construction of HMS *Victory* began in 1759 and took six years to complete. *Victory* was launched in 1765. After construction she spent most of the time inactive and in port.

The American Connection

Victory's first mission came in 1778, when she was sent to **engage** the French, who had allied with the rebellious American colonists. *Victory*'s first taste of war came close to the shores of Brittany, France, in the Battle of Ushant against a French fleet. The battle ended with no clear winner, but it would only be a matter of time before *Victory* made a name for herself as a first-class warship.

The British success at the Battle of Trafalgar earned HMS *Victory* a key honor in the Royal Navy.

Battle of Trafalgar

By the early 1800s, *Victory* was the flagship of Admiral Horatio Nelson (1758–1805). On October 21, 1805, the British fleet, commanded by Nelson, met a larger force of French and Spanish warships.

Did you know?

• During the 18th century, craftsmen who built ships were called **shipwrights**. An estimated 250 shipwrights worked on *Victory*.

• The Battle of Trafalgar took place during the Napoleonic Wars (1803-1815). In addition to losing Admiral Nelson, 57 men died and 102 were wounded on board *Victory*.

Credited as being the longest-serving ship in the Royal Navy, *Victory* is now docked in Portsmouth, England, where she is on display as a living piece of history.

Although the English had 27 **ships of the line** to the enemy's 33, they still managed to win the battle. Nelson captured or sank 17 enemy ships without losing a single British vessel. The victory, however, did not come without a cost. Hundreds of British sailors died in the battle, including Admiral Nelson, who was killed by enemy fire.

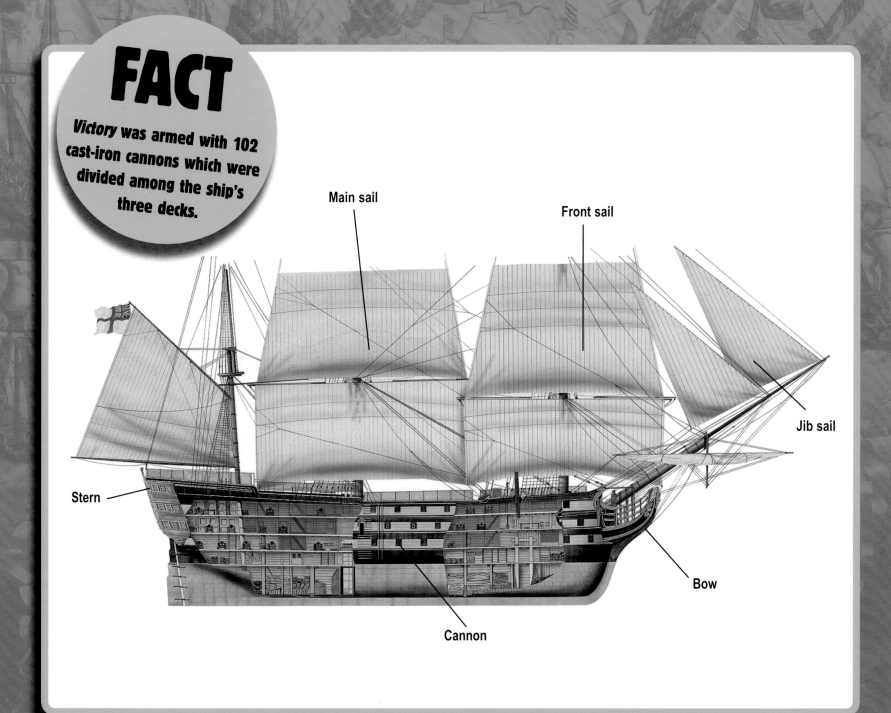

FACT

Victory was armed with 102 cast-iron cannons which were divided among the ship's three decks.

Main sail

Front sail

Jib sail

Stern

Cannon

Bow

Santísima Trinidad (1769)

Built on the Spanish-controlled island of Cuba in the 18th century, *Santísima Trinidad* was the largest ship of her time. She served the Spanish empire for over 30 years until surrendering to the British during the Battle of Trafalgar in 1805.

● ● ● ● ● ● ● ● ● ● ● ● ● ● ●

Santísima Trinidad was launched in 1769 and fought in many conflicts. Soon after Britain's thirteen American colonies declared their independence, *Santísima Trinidad* fought on the side of the American rebels. The Spanish ship of the line also fought against the British in the Napoleonic Wars.

Wind Power

Until the use of steam engines in the mid-19th century, most vessels that sailed the world's seas and oceans used wind energy as their main means

Santísima Trinidad had three masts that used huge sails as a means of propulsion and navigation.

A full-sized replica of the *Santísima Trinidad* can be seen docked in the harbor of Alicante, Spain.

British in the Battle of Trafalgar (1805). Unable to maneuver fast enough due to her large size, the Spanish warship became a target of several British ships. After receiving a great deal of damage that included the destruction of her masts, the ship's commander surrendered to the captain of HMS *Neptune*. Although the victorious British tried to save *Santísima Trinidad* in hopes of adding her to the Royal Navy, the damage was too great and she sank a day later.

of propulsion. Warships and **merchant ships** were built with tall masts and sails to capture the wind, allowing them to "set sail." One strategy used in naval battles was to destroy the enemy ship's masts, leaving the ship unable to maneuver and defenseless against an attack.

Surrender to HMS *Neptune*

Santísima Trinidad was part of a combined Spanish and French force that fought against the

Did you know?

• • • • • • • • • • • • • • •

• *Santísima Trinidad* was a little over 200 feet (61 m) long and had a crew of 1,000 men.

• *Santísima Trinidad* almost met her fate at the Battle of Cape St. Vincent (1797). Luckily, both crew and ship were rescued.

FACT

Santísima Trinidad's armament included over 130 cannons.

Main sail

Bowsprit

Rudder

Gun port

Cannon

Mast

26

USS Essex (1799)

USS *Essex* was one of the first ships built by the U.S. Navy to defend the young nation, which had recently won independence from British rule.

Construction of the 32-gun American **frigate** started in 1798. She was launched in 1799 and served the United States in battles against the French, North African pirates, and the British Royal Navy. USS *Essex* was also the first American warship to cross the Equator and travel as far as the Pacific and Indian Oceans.

The Barbary States

One of the first threats faced by the United States came from half a world away. Pirates from the **Barbary States** of North Africa were attacking American merchant ships on the Mediterranean Sea. Often forced to pay large **ransoms** for

Essex was one of the first warships built by the U.S. Navy. It served the newly formed nation in distant battles.

Did you know?

• • • • • • • • • • • •

- **USS *Essex* was named after the county where it was built, Essex County, Massachusetts.**

- **Facing the superior firepower of HMS *Phoebe*, *Essex* lost almost half her crew of 155 men.**

The War of 1812

Soon after war was declared against Britain, USS *Essex* sailed south, attacking British merchant and whaling ships in the South Atlantic Ocean and along the coast of Brazil. During this period, *Essex* captured over a dozen English ships. Her luck, however, would soon run out. On March 18, 1814, *Essex* met the British warship HMS *Phoebe* off the coast Chile. After a two-and-a-half hour battle, the American frigate was captured and put into service in the Royal Navy.

captured ships and crew, the United States finally took action by sending its small navy to put an end to these attacks. In addition to fighting in America's first foreign battles, USS *Essex* also remained in the region, escorting American merchant ships and protecting them from pirate attacks.

Once the British captured *Essex*, they added the ship to the Royal Navy where she served for a number of years.

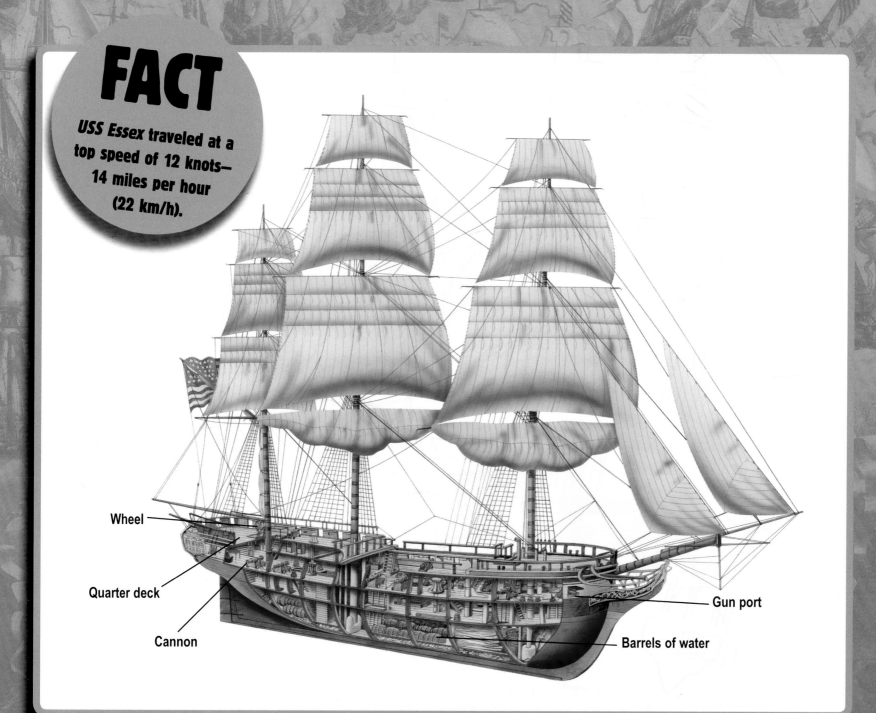

FACT

USS Essex traveled at a top speed of 12 knots— 14 miles per hour (22 km/h).

Wheel

Quarter deck

Cannon

Gun port

Barrels of water

Gloire (1859)

Built in the 1850s, and designed as a response to more powerful weapons, *Gloire* was France's first armored warship. With the introduction of the ironclad *Gloire* into the French navy, all other wooden warships became out-of-date.

By the middle of the 19th century, the age of the wooden warship was coming to an end. Starting with the Crimean War (1853–1856), nations around the world, including Britain, France, Russia, and the United States, began building **armored** ships in an attempt to defend against larger and more powerful weapons.

Ironclad Ships

Although *Gloire* is referred to as the first ironclad warship, she was still constructed using mostly wood. The armored plating that was added to the ship did not completely cover the vessel. Instead, it protected sections of the **hull** along the **waterline** and up to the guns that were mounted

Although *Gloire* was able to use steam to propel the ship, the captain often relied on wind power.

on a single deck. The armor plating was close to 5 inches (127 mm) thick.

From Wind Power to Steam Power

Much like earlier vessels, *Gloire* was built with tall masts capable of carrying huge sails. Propulsion, however, proved to be a problem. At the most, the ship was only able to reach a speed of 13 **knots** (15 mph; 24 km/h).

With the introduction of armored ships, the use of wind power was soon replaced by steam power. This new source of propulsion was

LA GLOIRE

Did you know?

• *Gloire* was **decommissioned** in 1879. Although she was protected by armor plating above water, the wooden section of the hull below water had rotted away.

• Soon after the British learned of the ironclad *Gloire*—which in English translates to "Glory"—they began constructing their own armored fleet.

produced by engines that burned coal to turn the propeller. However, modern ships were unlike earlier wind-driven vessels that could travel around the world without worrying about fuel. Steamships relied on coal and had limited space to store the fuel source. As a result, many of the early ironclad ships had a limited range of travel.

Unlike earlier wooden warships that carried guns on multiple decks, *Gloire*'s heavy guns were placed on just one deck.

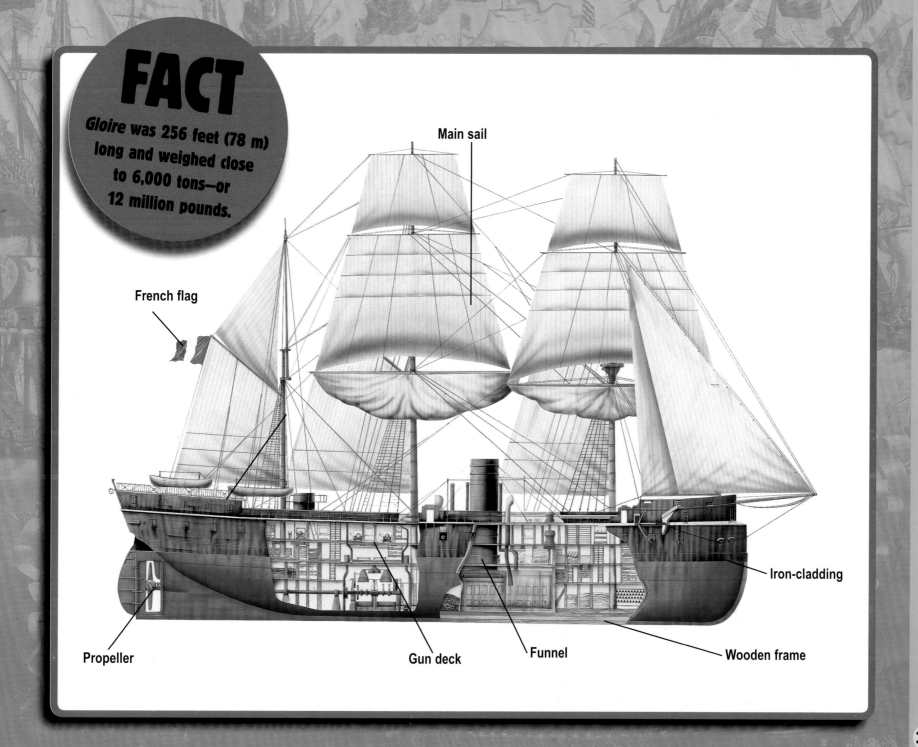

FACT

Gloire was 256 feet (78 m) long and weighed close to 6,000 tons—or 12 million pounds.

Main sail

French flag

Iron-cladding

Propeller

Gun deck

Funnel

Wooden frame

HMS Warrior (1861)

The Royal Navy vessel, HMS *Warrior* was built in response to France's introduction of the first armored warship, *Gloire*, in 1859. Construction for *Warrior* began in 1859. The ship was launched on December 29, 1860, and commissioned in 1861.

At the time, *Warrior* was the largest warship in the world. She weighed over 9,000 tons—or 18 million pounds (8 million kg)—and was 60 percent larger than *Gloire*.

Armament and Armor

All of the ship's 40 guns were mounted within her iron hull and kept on one deck. Most of the crew that operated the guns also lived on the same level and near the weapons that they were responsible for.

HMS *Warrior* is docked at the Portsmouth Historic Dockyard in England and is part of the National Museum of the Royal Navy.

Museum Ship

The ship was built during the reign of Queen Victoria, a time referred to as the Victorian era (1837–1901). Serving the Royal Navy for only 12 years, *Warrior* traveled to many distant lands in the British Empire and was part of a number of naval missions.

Over 150 years after her construction, HMS *Warrior* is still afloat and is part of the National Historic Fleet in Portsmouth, England.

Visitors are able to experience what life was like on HMS *Warrior*. She is one of the few surviving warships from the Victorian period of Britain's history.

The ship's armor was 5 inches (127 mm) thick and bolted onto the hull, which was made of iron with a tough **teak** wood backing that was able to better withstand enemy fire. Most of the vessel was protected by the iron armor, with the exception of the forward and aft ends.

Did you know?

• HMS *Warrior* was the first armored ship powered by wind (sail) as well as steam.

• Sixty-six men—called "stokers"— shoveled coal into the ship's furnaces, keeping the engines running. This was a hard and dirty job.

FACT

Warrior could carry 850 tons of coal.

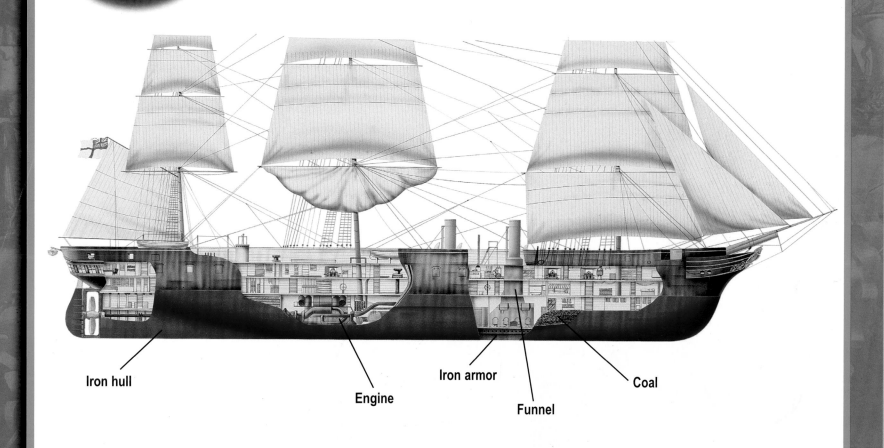

Iron hull

Engine

Iron armor

Funnel

Coal

CSS Virginia (1861)

The ironclad, CSS *Virginia*, was commissioned by the Confederate States of America in early 1862. She was built from a wooden Union warship captured by the Confederates. CSS *Virginia* fought against the U.S. (Union) Navy in the American Civil War.

In her brief time in the service of the Confederate navy, *Virginia* successfully faced off against five Union warships, doing serious damage to the Union navy.

Battle of Hampton Roads

Within a month after her commission in the Confederate navy, the ironclad *Virginia* attacked a group of Union ships that were part of the North Atlantic Blockade Squadron. During the battle, *Virginia* damaged a number of enemy warships and sank the frigate USS *Congress* after a failed attempt to take over the ship. The Confederate victory came at a huge cost to the U.S. Navy.

Virginia was destroyed on May 11, 1862, by her captain in an effort to keep the ship from falling into Union hands.

Realizing that the armored *Virginia* was a threat to the Union's wooden ships, Union naval commanders sent the ironclad, USS *Monitor*, to engage the enemy.

Did you know?

- **Originally designed by the U.S. Navy before the start of the American Civil War as a sailing frigate, the original name of the redesigned Confederate ironclad was *Merrimack*.**

- **In an effort to keep *Merrimack* from falling into enemy hands, Union forces unsuccessfully tried to sink the vessel. Once in Confederate hands, the ship was rebuilt as an ironclad and commissioned as the Confederate States Ship (CSS) *Virginia*.**

The two armored warships fought for over four hours with no clear victory in sight.

CSS *Virginia* vs. USS *Monitor*

One day after *Virginia*'s successful battle against the ships of the Union blockade, the Confederate warship faced off against the armored USS *Monitor*. This was the world's first battle between ironclad ships. After exchanging a number of shots, neither of the two vessels was able to gain an advantage. In the end, the battle was a draw, with neither ship able to claim victory.

FACT

The Union forces referred to *Virginia* by the nickname "The Rebel Monster."

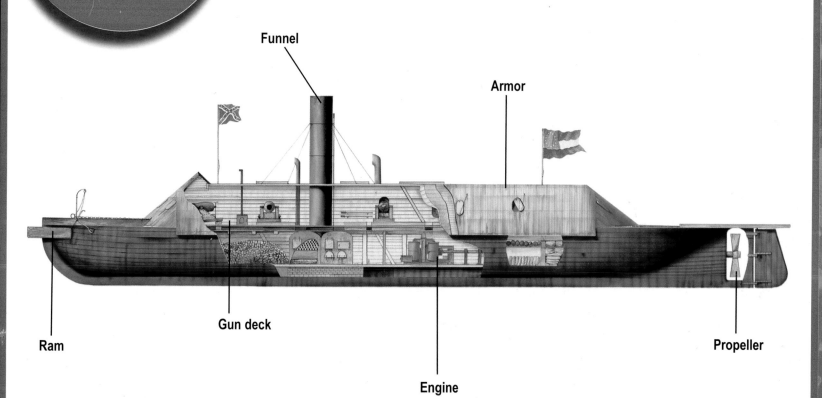

Funnel

Armor

Gun deck

Ram

Engine

Propeller

CSS Alabama (1862)

The wooden warship *Alabama* was built in Liverpool, England, thousands of miles away from where the American Civil War was being fought.

Alabama was 220 feet (67 m) long and carried a crew of 150 men. Her armament included fewer than a dozen guns. However, despite her size and weaponry, the Confederate raider caused a great deal of damage to the U.S. merchant fleet.

Commerce Raider

Alabama served less than two years in the Confederate navy. During this short period, she traveled from the shores of Europe to the northeast coast of the United States, from the Caribbean Sea to the tip of Africa, and on to the Indian and Pacific Oceans. Along the way, she captured or sank over 60 Union ships and took 2,000 prisoners. Her haul in ships and **cargo** was worth millions of dollars.

Captain Raphael Semmes on board *Alabama*.

CSS *Alabama* sank off the coast of Cherbourg, France.

Did you know?

• Although *Alabama* traveled far and wide, the ship and crew never docked in a Confederate port.

• As his ship sank, Captain Raphael Semmes was able to avoid Union capture. Along with 40 men of his crew, he was rescued by a British ship and taken to England, depriving the captain of USS *Kearsarge* of a formal surrender.

The Final Fight

After sailing back to Europe, *Alabama* soon faced the ironclad warship, USS *Kearsarge*, off the coast of France. In poor shape after being at sea for so long, and lacking the armor of the *Kearsarge*, *Alabama* was at a disadvantage. On June 19, 1864, just one hour after the battle began, *Alabama* was badly damaged. As the ship sank, *Kearsarge* was able to rescue 38 men from the burning vessel.

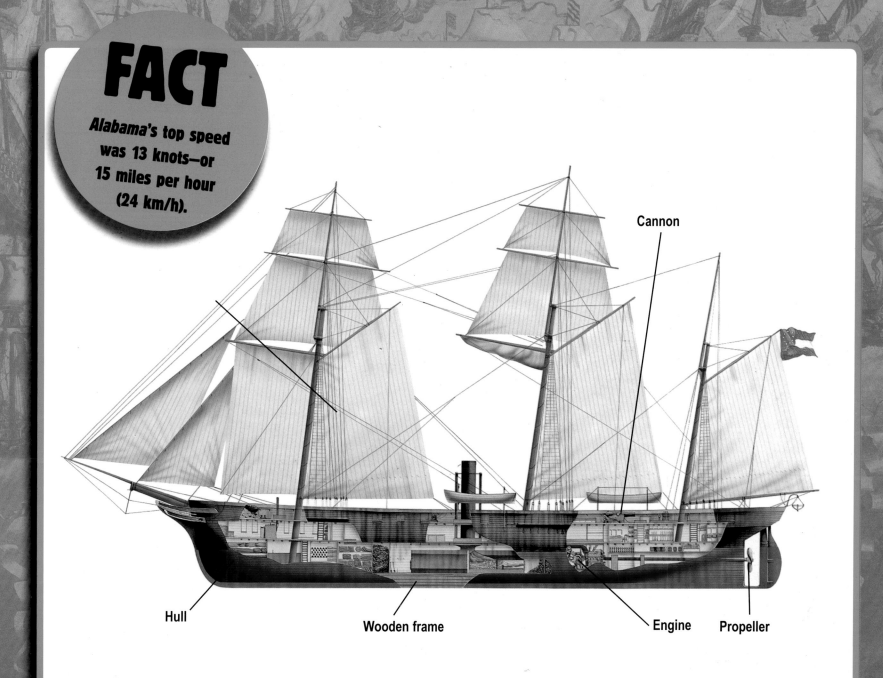

FACT

Alabama's top speed was 13 knots—or 15 miles per hour (24 km/h).

Cannon

Hull

Wooden frame

Engine

Propeller

Glossary

aft — the back part of a ship

armament — the weapons of a ship

armor — protective covering

Barbary States — loosely allied, independent states in North Africa that were known for their acts of piracy

cargo — goods carried by a ship, aircraft, or other vehicle

carrack — a long oceangoing ship built in the 15th and 16th centuries

commission — to officially enter a vessel into the navy

crew — all the people operating or serving aboard a ship

decommissioned — a ship that is officially removed from the navy

engage — to battle against or meet in a conflict

firepower — the strength of military weapons

flagship — the lead ship of a naval group that carries the commander

forward — the front part of a ship

frigate — a modern warship that is smaller than a destroyer

gun ports — the opening in a ship's hull from where the guns (cannons) open fire on an enemy

hull — the outer frame and shell of a ship

ironclad — early naval vessels protected in iron armor

knot — a unit of measurement used at sea to show speed traveled

launch — when a completed ship enters the water for the first time

mast — a long pole on a ship that supports the sails

merchant ship — a civilian ship used to carry cargo

murder hole — an opening from which defenders can fire on an enemy

propel — to move forward

ransoms — the release of a person or property in return for payment of a demanded price

ship of the line — a large naval warship with powerful guns used between the 17th and 19th centuries

shipwright — a builder of ships

surrender — to give up or give something over after a struggle

teak — a type of hardwood used to build ships

waterline — the point of the ship's hull that reaches the water

Index